The Old Debauchees. A Comedy by Henry Fielding

Henry Fielding was born at Sharpham Park, near Glastonbury, in Somerset on April 22nd 1707. His early years were spent on his parents' farm in Dorset before being educated at Eton.

An early romance ended disastrously and with it his removal to London and the beginnings of a glittering literary career; he published his first play, at age 21, in 1728.

He was prolific, sometimes writing six plays a year, but he did like to poke fun at the authorities. His plays were thought to be the final straw for the authorities in their attempts to bring in a new law. In 1737 The Theatrical Licensing Act was passed. At a stroke political satire was almost impossible. Fielding was rendered mute. Any playwright who was viewed with suspicion by the Government now found an audience difficult to find and therefore Theatre owners now toed the Government line.

Fielding was practical with the circumstances and ironically stopped writing to once again take up his career in the practice of law and became a barrister after studying at Middle Temple. By this time he had married Charlotte Craddock, his first wife, and they would go on to have five children. Charlotte died in 1744 but was immortalised as the heroine in both Tom Jones and Amelia.

Fielding was put out by the success of Samuel Richardson's Pamela, or Virtue Rewarded. His reaction was to spur him into writing a novel. In 1741 his first novel was published; the successful Shamela, an anonymous parody of Richardson's novel.

Undoubtedly the masterpiece of Fielding's career was the novel Tom Jones, published in 1749. It is a wonderfully and carefully constructed picaresque novel following the convoluted and hilarious tale of how a foundling came into a fortune.

Fielding was a consistent anti-Jacobite and a keen supporter of the Church of England. This led to him now being richly rewarded with the position of London's Chief Magistrate. Fielding continued to write and his career both literary and professional continued to climb.

In 1749 he joined with his younger half-brother John, to help found what was the nascent forerunner to a London police force, the Bow Street Runners. Fielding's ardent commitment to the cause of justice in the 1750s unfortunately coincided with a rapid deterioration in his health. Such was his decline that in the summer of 1754 he travelled, with Mary and his daughter, to Portugal in search of a cure. Gout, asthma, dropsy and other afflictions forced him to use crutches. His health continued to fail alarmingly.

Henry Fielding died in Lisbon two months later on October 8th, 1754.

As it is Acted at the THEATRE-ROYAL in DRURY-LANE.

By His MAJESTY's Servants.

By the Author of the MODERN HUSBAND.

Index of Contents

PROLOGUE

Spoken by Mr. William Mills.

I Wish, with all my Heart, the Stage and Town
Would both agree to cry all Prologues down;
That we, no more oblig'd to say or sing,
Might drop this useless necessary Thing:
No more with aukward Strut, before the Curtain,
Chaunt out some Rhimes—there's neither good nor hurt in.

What is this Stuff the Poets make us deal in,
But some old worn-out Jokes of their Retailing:
From Sages of our own, or former Times,
Transvers'd from Prose, perhaps transpros'd from Rhimes.

How long the Tragick Muse her Station kept,
How Guilt was humbl'd, and how Tyrants wept,
Forgetting still how often Hearers slept.

Perhaps, for Change, you, now and then, by Fits,
Are told that Criticks are the Bane of Wits;
How they turn Vampyres, being dead and damn'd,
And with the Blood of living Bards are cramm'd:
That Poets thus tormented die, and then
The Devil gets in them, and they suck agen.

Thus modern Bards, like Bays, their Prologues frame,
For this, and that, and every Play the same,
Which you, most justly, neither praise nor blame.

As something must be spoke, no matter what;
No Friends are now by Prologues lost or got;
By such Harangues we raise nor Spleen, nor Pity
Thus ends this idle, but important Ditty.

DRAMATIS PERSONAE

MEN

Old Laroon.	Mr. Shepard.
Young Laroon.	Mr. Mills, Junior.
Father Martin.	Mr. Cibber, Junior.
Old Jourdain.	Mr. Roberts.

WOMEN

| Isabel. | Miss Raftor. |
| Beatrice. | Miss Williams. |

SCENE - THOULON

ACT I. SCENE I

SCENE, Mr. Jourdain's

ISABEL, BEATRICE.

ISABEL - A Nunnery! Ha, ha, ha! And is it possible, my dear Beatrice, you can intend to sacrifice your Youth and Beauty, to go out of the World as soon as you come into it!

BEATRICE - No one, my dear Isabel, can sacrifice too much or too soon to Heaven.

ISABEL - Pshaw! Heaven regards Hearts and not Faces, and an old Woman will be as acceptable a Sacrifice as a young one.

BEATRICE - It is possible you may come to a better Understanding, and value the World as little as I do.

ISABEL - As you say, it is possible when I can enjoy it no longer, I may; nay, I do not care if I promise you when I grow old and ugly, I'll come and keep you Company: But this I am positive, till the World is weary of me, I never shall be weary of the World.

BEATRICE - What can a Woman of Sense see in it worth her valuing?

ISABEL - Oh! ten thousand pretty things! Equipage, Cards, Musick, Plays, Balls, Flattery, Visits, and that prettiest thing of all pretty things, a pretty Fellow—I rather wonder what Charms a Woman of any Spirit can fancy in a Nunnery, in watching, working, praying, and sometimes, I am afraid, wishing for other Company than that of an old fusty Friar—Oh! 'tis a delightful State, when every Man one sees, instead of tempting us to Sin, is to rebuke us for them.

BEATRICE - Such Sentiments as these would indeed make you very uneasy—but believe me, Child, you would soon bring yourself to hate Mankind; fasting and praying are the best Cures in the World for these violent Passions.

ISABEL - On my Conscience I should want neither; if the continual Sight of a Set of dirty Priests would not bring me to abhor Mankind, I dare swear nothing could.

SCENE II

OLD LAROON, ISABEL, BEATRICE.

OLD LAROON - Good-morrow, my little Wag-tail—my Grashopper, my Butterfly. Odso! you little Baggage, you look as full of—as full of Love and Sport and Wantonness—I wish I was a young Fellow again—Oh! that I was but five and twenty for thy sake. Where's my Boy? What, has not he been with you, has not he serenaded you? Odsheart—I never let his Mother sleep for a Month before I married her.

ISABEL - Indeed!

OLD LAROON - No Madam, nor for a Month afterwards neither. The young Fellows of this Age are nothing, mere Butterflies, to those of ours—Odsheart I remember the Time, when I could have taken a Hop, Step, and Jump over the Steeple of Notre Dame.

BEATRICE - I fancy the Sparks of your Age had Wings, Sir.

OLD LAROON - Wings, you little Baggage, no—but they had—they had Limbs, like Elephants, and as strong they were as Sampson, and as swift as—Why, I have my self run down a Stag in a fair Chace, and eat him afterwards for my Dinner. But come, where is my old Neighbour, my old Friend, my old Jourdain?

ISABEL - At his Devotions, I suppose, this is the Hour he generally employs in them.

OLD LAROON - This Hour! ay, all Hours. I dare swear he spends more Time in them, than all the Priests in Toulon. Well, give him his due, he was wicked as long as he could be so, and when he could sin no longer, why he began to repent that he had sinned at all. Oh! there is nothing so devout as an old Whoremaster.

BEATRICE - I fancy then it will be shortly Time for you to think of it, Sir!

OLD LAROON - Ay, Madam, about some thirty or forty Years hence it may—Odsheart! I am but in the prime of my Years yet: And if it was not for a saucy young Rascal who looks me in the Face and calls me Father, might make a very good Figure among the Beaus. But tho' I am not so young in Years, I am in Constitution as any of them; and I don't question but to live to see a Son and a great Grandson both born on the same Day.

ISABEL - You will excuse this Lady, Mr. Laroon, who is going to retire so much earlier—

OLD LAROON - Retire! Then it is with a young Fellow, I hope.

ISABEL - Into a Cloister, I assure you.

OLD LAROON - A Cloister! Why, Madam, if you have a mind to hang your self at the Year's End; would it not be better to spend your Time in Matrimony than in a Nunnery? Don't let a Set of rascally Priests put strange Notions in your Head. Take my Word for it, and I am a very honest Fellow, there are no Raptures worth a Louse, but those in the Arms of a brisk young Cavalier. Of all the Actions of my Youth, there are none I reflect on with so much Pleasure as having burnt half a Dozen Nunneries, and delivered several hundred Virgins out of Captivity.

BEATRICE - Oh! Villany! unheard of Villany!

ISABEL - Unheard of till this Moment I dare swear.

OLD LAROON - Out of which Number there are at present nine Countesses, three Dutchesses, and a Queen, who owe their Liberty and their Promotion to this Arm.

SCENE III

OLD LAROON, YOUNG LAROON, ISABEL, BEATRICE.

OLD LAROON - You are a fine Spark truly to let your Father visit your Mistress before you—'Sdeath! I believe you are no Son of mine. Where have you been, Sir? What have you been doing, Sir, hey?

YOUNG LAROON - Sir, I have been at my Devotions.

OLD LAROON - At your Devotions! nay, then you are no Son of mine, that's certain. Is not this the Shrine you are to offer up at, Sirrah! Is not here the Altar you are to officiate at? Sirrah! you have no Blood of mine in you. I believe you are the Bastard of some travelling English Alderman, and must have come into the World with a Custard in your Mouth.

YOUNG LAROON - I hope, Madam, you will allow my Excuse, tho' the old Gentleman here will not.

OLD LAROON - Old Gentleman! very fine! Sirrah! I'll convince you I am a young Gentleman; I'll marry to-night, and make you a Brother before you are a Father; I'll teach you to thrust him out of the World that thrust you into it—Madam, have no more to say to the ungracious Dog.

YOUNG LAROON - That will be a sure way to quit all Obligations between us; for the Happiness I propose in this Lady, is the chief Reason why I should thank you for bringing me into the World.

OLD LAROON - What's that you say, Sir; say that again, Sir.

YOUNG LAROON - I was only thanking you, Sir, for desiring this Lady to take from me all I esteem on Earth.

OLD LAROON - Well enough that! I begin to think him my own again. I have made that very Speech to half the Women in Paris.

SCENE IV

To them MARTIN.

MARTIN - Peace be with you all, Good People.

OLD LAROON - Peace cannot stay long in any Place where a Priest comes.
[Aside.

MARTIN - Daughter, I am ready to receive your Confession—

OLD LAROON - Ay, ay, she has a fine Parcel of sinful Thoughts to answer for, I warrant her.

MARTIN - Mr. Laroon, you are too much inclined to Slander, I must reprove you for it. My Daughter's Thoughts are as pure as a Saint's.

OLD LAROON - As any Saint's in Christendom within a Day of Matrimony.

MARTIN - Within a Day of Matrimony; it is too quick; I have not yet had sufficient Time to prepare her Mind for that solemn Sacrament.

OLD LAROON - Prepare her Mind for a young Fellow; prepare your Mind for a Bishoprick.

MARTIN - Sir, there are Ceremonies requisite, I shall be as expeditious as possible, but the Church has Rules.

OLD LAROON - Sir, you may be as expeditious or as slow as you please, but I will not have my Boy disappointed of his Happiness one Day, for all the Rules in Europe.

SCENE V

MARTIN, ISABEL.

MARTIN - I shall bring this Haughtiness to a Penance, you may not like. Well, my dear Daughter, I hope your Account is not long. You have not many Articles since our last Reckoning.

ISABEL - I wish you do not think it so, Father. First, telling nine Lyes at the Opera the other Night to Mr. Laroon; yesterday talk'd during the whole Mass to a young Cavalier, [he groans.] Nay, if you groan already, I shall make you groan more before I have done; last Night cheated at Cards, scandalized three of my Acquaintance, went to Bed without saying my Prayers, and dreamt of Mr. Laroon.

MARTIN - Oh! Tell me the Particulars of that Dream.

ISABEL - Nay, Father, that I must be excus'd.

MARTIN - Modesty at Confession is as unseasonable as in Bed, and your Mind should appear as naked to your Confessor, as your Person to your Husband.

ISABEL - I thought he embraced me with the utmost Tenderness.

MARTIN - But were you pleased therewith?

ISABEL - You know, Father, a Lye now would be the greatest of Sins. I was not displeased I assure you. But I have often heard you say, there is no Sin in Love.

MARTIN - No, in Love it self there is not: Love is not Malum in se. Nor in the Excess is there sometimes any: but then it must be rightly placed, must be directed to a proper Object. The Love a Daughter bears her Confessor is no doubt not only innocent, but extremely laudable.

ISABEL - Yes, but that—that is another sort of Love, you know.

MARTIN - You are deceived, there is but one sort of Love which is justifiable, or, indeed, desirable.

ISABEL - I hope my Love for Laroon is that.

MARTIN - That I know not, I wish it may; however, I have some Dispute as yet remaining with me concerning it; 'till that be satisfied, it will be improper for you to proceed any farther in the Affair. All the Penance, therefore, I shall enjoin you on this Confession, is to defer your Marriage one Week; by which time I shall have resolved within my self whether you shall marry him at all.

ISABEL - Not marry him at all? Sure, Father, you are not in earnest.

MARTIN - I never jest on these Occasions.

ISABEL - What Reason can you have?

MARTIN - My Reasons may not be so ripe for your Ears at present. But, perhaps, better things are designed for you.

ISABEL - A Fidlestick! I tell you, Father, better things cannot be designed for me. I suppose, you have found out some old Fellow with twenty Livres a Year more in his Power; but I can assure you, if I marry not Laroon, I'll not marry any.

MARTIN - Perhaps you are not designed to marry any. Let me feel your Pulse—Extremely feverish.

ISABEL - You are enough to put any one in a Fever. I was to have been married to-morrow to a pretty Fellow, and now I must defer my Marriage, 'till you have consider'd whether I shall marry at all or no.

MARTIN - Have you any more Sins to confess!

ISABEL - Sins! You have put all my Sins out of my Head, I think.

MARTIN – Benedicite [crossing himself.] Daughter, you shall see me soon again, for great things are in Agitation; At present, I leave you to your Prayers.

SCENE VI

ISABEL alone.

ISABEL - Sure never poor Maid had more need of Prayers: but you have left me no great Stomach to them. Great things are in Agitation! What can he mean? It must be so—Some old liquorish Rogue with a Title, or a larger Estate hath a mind to supplant my dear Laroon.

SCENE VII

YOUNG LAROON, ISABEL.

YOUNG LAROON - My Isabel, my Sweet! How painfully do I count each tedious Hour, till I can call you mine?

ISABEL - Indeed, you are like to count many more tedious Hours than you imagine.

YOUNG LAROON - Ha! What means my Love?

ISABEL - I would not have your Wishes too impatient, that's all; but if you will wait a Week, you shall know whether I intend to marry you or not.

YOUNG LAROON - And is this possible? Can Words like these fall from Isabel's sweet Lips; can she be false, inconstant, perjured?

ISABEL - Oh! do not discharge such a Volley of terrible Names upon me before you are certain I deserve them; doubt only whether I can be obedient to my Confessor, and guess the rest.

YOUNG LAROON - Can he have enjoined you to be perjured, by Heaven it would be sinful to obey him.

ISABEL - Be satisfied, if I prevail with my self to obey him in this Week's Delay, I will carry my Obedience no farther.

YOUNG LAROON - Oh! to what Happiness have those dear Words restor'd me. I am again my self: for while the Possession of thee is sure, tho' distant, there is in that dear Hope, more Transport than any other actual Enjoyment can afford.

ISABEL - Well adieu, and to cram you quite full with Hope (since you like the Food) I here promise you, that the Commands of all the Priests in France shall not force me to marry another. That is, Sir, I will either marry you or die a Maid, and I have no violent Inclination to the latter, on the Word of a Virgin.

SCENE VIII

YOUNG LAROON solus.

Whether a violent Hatred to my Father, or an inordinate Love for Mischief, hath set the Priest on this Affair, I know not. Perhaps it is the former—for the old Gentleman hath the Happiness of being universally hated by every Priest in Toulon—Let a Man abuse a Physician, he makes another Physician his Friend, let him rail at a Lawyer, another will plead his Cause gratis; if he libel this Courtier, that Courtier receives him into his Bosom: but let him once attack a Hornet or a Priest, the whole Nest of Hornets, and the whole Regiment of Black-guards are sure to be upon him.

SCENE IX

OLD LAROON laughing, YOUNG LAROON.

YOUNG LAROON - You are merry, Sir.

OLD LAROON - Merry, Sir! Ay, Sir! I am merry, Sir. Would you have your Father sad, you Rascal? Have you a mind to bury him in his Youth?

YOUNG LAROON - Pardon me, Sir, I rather wished to know the happy Occasion of your Mirth.

OLD LAROON - The Occasion of my Mirth, Sir, is the saddest Sight that ever Mortal beheld.

YOUNG LAROON - A very odd Occasion indeed.

OLD LAROON - Very odd truly. It is the Sight of an old honest Whoremaster in a Fit of Despair, and a damned Rogue of a Priest riding him to the Devil.

YOUNG LAROON - Ay, Sir, but I have seen a more melancholy Sight.

OLD LAROON - Ha! what can that be?

YOUNG LAROON - A fine young Lady in a Fit of Love, and a Priest keeping her from her Lover.

OLD LAROON - How?

YOUNG LAROON - The Explanation of which is, that Father Martin hath put off our Match for a Week.

OLD LAROON - Put off your Match with Isabel!

YOUNG LAROON - Even so, Sir.

OLD LAROON - Well I never have made a Hole in a Gown yet, I never have tapped a Priest: but if I don't let out some reverend Blood before the Sun sets, may I never See him rise again. I'll carbonade the Villain, I'll make a Ragout for the Devil's Supper of him.

YOUNG LAROON - Let me intreat you, Sir, to do nothing rashly, as long as I am safe in the Faith of my Isabel.

OLD LAROON - I tell you, Sirrah, no Man is safe in the Faith of a Mistress, no one is secure of a Woman till he is in Bed with her. Had there been any Security in the Faith of a Mistress, I had been at present married to half the Dutchesses in France. I no more rely on what a Woman says out of a Church, than on what a Priest says in it.

YOUNG LAROON - Pardon me, Sir: but I should have very little Appetite to marry the Woman whom I had such an Opinion of.

OLD LAROON - You had an Opinion of! What Business have you to have any Opinion. Is it not enough that I have an Opinion of her, that is of her Fortune—But I suppose you are one of those romantick, whining Coxcombs, that are in Love with a Woman behind her Back: Sirrah, I have had two Women lawfully, and two thousand unlawfully, and never was in Love in my Life.

YOUNG LAROON - Well, Sir, then I am happy, that we both agree in the same Person; I like the Woman, and you her Fortune.

OLD LAROON - Yes, you Dog, and I'd have you secure her as soon as you can: for if a greater Fortune should be found out in Toulon, I'd make you marry her—So go find out your Mistress, and stick close to her, and I'll go seek the Priest, whom, if I can find, I will stick close to with a Vengeance.

SCENE X - Another Apartment

JOURDAIN, MARTIN.

JOURDAIN - Alas! Father, there is one Sin sticks by me more than any I have confessed to you. It is so enormous a one my Shame hath prevented me discovering it—I have often concealed my Crimes from my Confessor.

MARTIN - That is a damnable Sin indeed. It seemeth to argue a Distrust of the Church, the greatest of all Crimes; a Sin I fear the Church cannot forgive.

JOURDAIN - Oh! say not so, Father!

MARTIN - I should have said will not, or not without difficulty: for the Church can do all things.

JOURDAIN - That is some Comfort again.

MARTIN - I hope, however, tho' you have not confessed them, you have not forgotten them; for they must be confessed before they can be forgiven.

JOURDAIN - I hope I shall recollect them, they are a black Roll—I remember I once was the Occasion of ruining a Woman's Reputation by shewing a Letter from her.

MARTIN - If you had shewn it to the Priest it had been no Fault.

JOURDAIN - Alas! Sir, I wrote the Letter to my self, and thus traduced the Innocent. I afterwards commanded a Company of Granadiers, at the taking of a Town, where I knocked a poor old Gentleman in the Head for the sake of his Money, and ravished his Daughter.

MARTIN - These are crying Sins indeed.

JOURDAIN - At the same time I robbed a Jesuit of two Pistoles.

MARTIN - Oh! damnable! Oh! execrable!

JOURDAIN - Good Father, have Patience: I once borrowed five hundred Livres of an honest Citizen in Paris, and repay'd him by lying with his Wife: And what sits nearest my Heart, was forced to pay a young Cavalier the same Sum, by suffering him to lie with mine.

MARTIN - Oh!

JOURDAIN - And yet what are these to what I have done since I commenced Merchant. What have I not done to get a Penny. I insured a Ship for a great Value, and then cast it away; I broke when I was worth a hundred thousand Livres, and went over to London. I settled there, renounced my Religion, and was made a Justice of Peace.

MARTIN - Oh! that Seat of Heresy and Damnation! that Whore of Babylon!

JOURDAIN - With the Whores of Babylon did I unite: I protected them from Justice: Gaming-houses and Baudy-houses did I license, nay, and frequent too; I never punished any Vice but Poverty: for Oh! I dread to name it: I once committed a Priest to Newgate for picking Pockets.

MARTIN - Oh! monstrous! horrible! dreadful! I'll hear no more. Thou art damn'd without Reprieve.

JOURDAIN - Take Pity, Father, take Pity on a Penitent.

MARTIN - Pity! the Church abhors it. 'Twere Mercy to such a Wretch to pray him into Purgatory.

JOURDAIN - I'll give all my Estate to the Church, I'll found Monasteries, I'll build Abbies.

MARTIN - All will not do, ten thousand Masses will not deliver you.

JOURDAIN - Was ever such a miserable Wretch!

MARTIN - Thou hast Sins enough to damn thy whole Family. Monstrous Impiety! to lift up the Hand of Justice against the Church.

JOURDAIN - Oh speak some Comfort to me: will no Penance expiate my Crime?

MARTIN - It is too grievous for a single Penance, go settle your Estate on the Church, and send your Daughter to a Nunnery, her Prayers will avail more than yours: Heaven hears the young and innocent with Pleasure. I will, my self, say four Masses a-day for you; and all these, I hope, will purchase your Forgiveness, at least your Stay in Purgatory will be short.

JOURDAIN - My Daughter! She is to be married to-morrow, and I shall never prevail on her.

MARTIN - You must force her; your all depends on it.

JOURDAIN - But I have already sworn I will not force her.

MARTIN - The Church absolves you from that Oath, and it were now Impiety to keep it. Go, lose not a Moment, see her entered with the utmost Expedition; she may put it out of your Power.

JOURDAIN - What a poor miserable Wretch am I?

SCENE XI

MARTIN solus.

Thou art a miserable Wretch indeed! And it is on such miserable Wretches depends our Power: that Superstition which tears thy Bowels, feeds ours. This Nunnery is a Master-piece, let me but once shut up my dear Isabel from every other Man, and the Warmth of her Constitution may be my very powerful Friend. How far am I got already from the very Brink of Despair, by the Despair of this old Fool. Superstition, I adore thee,

Thou handle to the cheated Layman's Mind,
By which in Fetters Priestcraft leads Mankind.

ACT II. SCENE I

JOURDAIN, ISABEL.

JOURDAIN -Have you no Compassion for your Father, for him that gave you being? Could you bear to hear me howl in Purgatory?

ISABEL - Lud! Pappa! Do you think your putting me into Purgatory in this World, will save you from Purgatory in the next? If you have any Sins you must repent of them your self; for I give you my Word, I have enough to do to repent of my own.

JOURDAIN - You will soon wipe off that Score, and will be then in a Place where you cannot contract a new one.

ISABEL - Indeed, Sir, to shut a Woman out from Sin is not so easy. But, dear Sir, how can it enter into your Head, that my Penance can be acceptable for your Sin? Take my Word, one Week's fasting will be of more Service to you than this long Fast you would enjoin me.

JOURDAIN - Alas! Child, if fasting would do, I am sure I have not been wanting to my Duty: I have fasted till I am almost worn away to nothing; I have almost fasted my self into Purgatory, while I was fasting my self out of it.

ISABEL - But whence comes all this Apprehension of your Danger?

JOURDAIN - Whence should it come, but from the Church.

ISABEL - Oh! Sir, I have thought of the most lucky thing. You know, my Cousin Beatrice is just going into a Nunnery, and she will pray for you as much as you would have her.

JOURDAIN - Trifle not with so serious a Concern. No Prayers but yours will ever do me good.

ISABEL - Then you shall have them any where but in a Nunnery.

JOURDAIN - They must be there too.

ISABEL - That will be impossible: for if I was there, instead of praying you out of Purgatory, my Prayers would be all bent to pray my self out of the Nunnery again.

SCENE II

OLD LAROON, JOURDAIN, ISABEL.

OLD LAROON - A Dog, a Villain, put off my Son's Match. Mr. Jourdain, your Servant; will you suffer a Rogue of a Jesuit to defer your Daughter's Marriage a whole Week?

JOURDAIN - I am sorry, Mr. Laroon, for the Disappointment, but her Marriage will be deferred longer than that.

OLD LAROON - How, Sir!

JOURDAIN - She is intended for another Marriage, Sir, a much better Match.

OLD LAROON - A much better Match!

ISABEL - Yes, Sir, I am to be sent to a Nunnery, to pray my Father out of Purgatory.

OLD LAROON - Oh! Ho! We'll make that Matter very easy: he shall have no Fear of Purgatory; for I'll send him to the Devil this Moment. Come, Sir, draw, draw—

JOURDAIN - Draw what, Sir!

OLD LAROON - Draw your Sword, Sir.

JOURDAIN - Alas, Sir, I have long since done with Swords, I have broke my Sword long since.

OLD LAROON - Then I shall break your Head, you old Rogue.

JOURDAIN - Heyday—you are mad; what's the Matter?

OLD LAROON - Oh! no matter, no matter, you have used me ill, and you are a Son of a Whore, that's all.

JOURDAIN - I wou'd not, Mr. Laroon, have my Conscience accuse me of using you ill: I would not have preferred any earthly Match to your Son, but if Heaven requires her—

OLD LAROON - I shall run mad.

JOURDAIN - I hope my Daughter has Grace enough to make an Atonement for her Father's Sins.

OLD LAROON - And so, you wou'd atone for all your former Rogueries, by a greater, by perverting the Design of Nature! Was this Girl intended for praying! Hearkee, old Gentleman, let the young Couple together, and they'll sacrifice their first Fruits to the Church.

JOURDAIN - It is impossible.

OLD LAROON - Well, Sir, then I shall attempt to persuade you no longer; so, Sir, I desire you would fetch your Sword.

SCENE III

YOUNG LAROON in a Friar's Habit, OLD LAROON, JOURDAIN.

YOUNG LAROON - Let Peace be in this House—Where is the Sinner Jourdain?

JOURDAIN - Here is the miserable Wretch.

OLD LAROON - Death and the Devil, another Priest.

YOUNG LAROON - Then know I am thy Friend, and am come to save thee from Destruction.

OLD LAROON - That's likely enough.

YOUNG LAROON - St. Francis the Patron of our Order hath sent me on this Journey, to caution thee, that thou may not suffer thy sinful Daughter to profane the holy Veil. Such was it seems thy Purpose; but the Perdition that would have attended it I dread to think on. Rejoice therefore, and prostrate thy self at the Shrine of a Saint, who has not only sent thee this Caution, but does himself intercede for all thy Sins.

OLD LAROON - Agad! and St. Francis is a very honest Fellow, and thou art the first Priest that ever I lik'd in my whole Life.

JOURDAIN - St. Francis honours me too much. I shall try to deserve the Favour of that Saint. But wherefore is my Daughter denied the holy Veil?

YOUNG LAROON - Your Daughter, I am concerned to say it, is now with Child by a young Gentleman, one Mr. Laroon.

JOURDAIN - Oh Heavens!

OLD LAROON - What's that you say, Sir, because I thought I heard somewhat of a damn'd Lye come out of your Mouth.

YOUNG LAROON - Sir, it is St. Francis speaks within me, and he cannot be mistaken.

OLD LAROON - I can tell you, Sir, if that young Gentleman had heard you, he would certainly have thrashed St. Francis out of you.

YOUNG LAROON - Sir, you have nothing to do now, but to prepare the Match with the utmost Expedition.

OLD LAROON - This St. Francis must lye, or the Boy would not be so eager upon the Affair: No one is ever eager to sign Articles when they have entered the Town. Well, Master Jourdain, if the young Dog has tripped up your Daughter's Heels in an unlawful way, as St. Francis says, why, he shall make her amends and—and do it in a lawful one. So I'll go see for my Son, while you go and comfort the poor Chicken that is pining for fear of a Nunnery. Odsheart, it would be very hard indeed, when a Girl has once had her Belly full, that she must fast all her Life afterwards.

YOUNG LAROON - I have deliver'd my Commission and shall now return to my Convent—Farewel, and return Thanks to St. Francis.

JOURDAIN - Oh! St. Francis! St. Francis! What a merciful Saint art thou!

SCENE IV

Another Apartment.

MARTIN, ISABEL.

MARTIN - Indeed, Child, there are Pleasures in a retired Life, which you are entirely ignorant of. Nay, there are Indulgencies granted to People in that State, which would be sinful out of it. And, perhaps, the same Liberties are permitted them with one Person, which are deny'd them with another. Come, put on a chearful Countenance, you don't know what you are design'd for.

ISABEL - No, but I know what I am not design'd for.

MARTIN - Let me feel your Pulse.

ISABEL - You are a Physician as well as a Priest, I suppose.

MARTIN - Have you never any odd Dreams?

ISABEL - No.

MARTIN - Do you never find any strange Emotions?

ISABEL - No. None but what I believe are very natural.

MARTIN - Strange that! Did you never see me in your Sleep?

ISABEL - I never dream of a Priest, I assure you.

MARTIN - Nay, nay; be candid, confess, perhaps, there may be nothing so sinful in it. We cannot help what we are design'd for. We are only passive, and the Sin lies not at our Doors. While you are only passive, I'll answer for your Sins.

ISABEL - What do you mean?

MARTIN - That you must not yet know—Great things are design'd for you, very great things are designed for you.

ISABEL - (Hum! I begin to guess what is design'd for me.)   [Aside.

MARTIN - Those Eyes have a Fire in them that scarce seems mortal. Come hither—give me a Kiss—ha! there is a Sweetness in that Breath like what I've read of Ambrosia. That Bosom heaves like those of Priestesses of old, when big with Inspiration.

ISABEL - (Haity-tity—Are you thereabouts good Father?)   [Aside.

MARTIN - Let me embrace thee, my dear Daughter, let me give thee Joy of such Promotion, such Happiness as will attend you.

ISABEL - I'll try this reverend Gentleman his own way.   [Aside.

MARTIN - You must resign your self up to my Will, you must be passive in all things.

ISABEL - Oh! let me thus beg Pardon, on my Knees, for an Offence which Modesty occasioned.

MARTIN - Ha! speak.

ISABEL - Oh! I see it is in vain to hide my Secrets from you. What need have I to confess what you already know?

MARTIN - Confession was intended for the sake of the Penitent, not the Confessor: for to the Church all things are revealed.

ISABEL - Oh! then I had a Dream—I dreamt—I dreamt—oh! I can never tell you what I dreamt.

MARTIN - Horrible!

ISABEL - I dreamt—I dreamt—I dreamt—

MARTIN - Oh! the Strength of Sin!

ISABEL - I dreamt I was brought to bed of the Pope.

MARTIN - The very Happiness I meant, let me embrace you, let me kiss you, my dear Daughter: Henceforth you may defy Purgatory—the Mother of a Pope was never there.

ISABEL - But how can that be, when I am to be a Nun, Father?

MARTIN - Leave the Means to me. Learn only to be passive, the Church will work the rest. A Pope is always the Son of a Nun. Go you to your Chamber, wash your self, then pray devoutly, shut every Ray of Light out, leave open the Door and expect the Consequence.

ISABEL - Father, I shall be obedient—oh! the Villain!

MARTIN - Be passive and be happy.

SCENE V

JOURDAIN, MARTIN, ISABEL.

MARTIN - Ha! Why this unseasonable Interruption, while your Daughter is at Confession?

JOURDAIN - Oh, Father, I have brought you News will make you happy, will rejoice your poor Heart. My Daughter is redeemed.

MARTIN - Out of Purgatory—vain Man! dost thou think to inform the Church?

JOURDAIN - I suppose St. Francis has been beforehand with me. Indeed I should have imagined that before: for we seldom hear any thing from the Saints, but thro' the Mouth of a Priest.

MARTIN - (What does he mean?)   [Aside.

JOURDAIN - Well, Daughter, the Thoughts of a Nunnery now give you no Uneasiness.

MARTIN - No, no, she is perfectly reconciled to it, and I am confident, would not quit the Nunnery for the Bed of a Prince.

JOURDAIN - Ha! would not quit the Nunnery, Heaven forbid.

MARTIN - How! you are not mad!

JOURDAIN - Unless with Joy. I thought you had known that I have received an Order from St. Francis, to marry my Daughter immediately.

MARTIN - Oh! Folly! to marry her immediately; why ay, to marry her to the Church, St. Francis means. You see into what Errors the Laity run, when they go without the Leading-strings of the Church, and would interpret for themselves what they know nothing of.

ISABEL - I'll take this Opportunity to steal off, and communicate a Design of mine to young Laroon, which may draw this Priest into a Snare he little dreams of.

JOURDAIN - But I cannot see how that should be St. Francis's Meaning: For tho' my Daughter may be married to the Church in a figurative Sense, sure, she cannot be with Child by the Church in a literal one.

MARTIN - I see the Business now, unhappy Man! I was in Hopes to have prevented this—Exorcizo te, Exorcizo te, Satan. Ton Dapamibominos prosephe podas ocus Achilleus.

JOURDAIN - Bless us, what mean you?

MARTIN - You are possessed; the Devil has taken possession of you; he is now within you, I saw him just now look out of your Eyes.

JOURDAIN - O miserable Wretch that I am!

SCENE VI

OLD LAROON, YOUNG LAROON, JOURDAIN, MARTIN.

OLD LAROON - Mr. Jourdain, your Servant. Where is my Daughter-in-law! I'll warrant she will easily forgive one Day's forwarding the Match. Odso, it's an Error of the right side.

JOURDAIN - Talk not to me of my Daughter, I am possessed, I am possessed.

OLD LAROON - Possessed—what the Devil are you possessed with.

JOURDAIN - I am possessed with the Devil.

OLD LAROON - You are possessed with a Priest, and that's worse. Come, let's have the Wedding, and at Night, we'll drive the Devil out of you with a Fidle. The Devil is a great Lover of Musick. I have known half a Dozen Devils dance out of a Man's Mouth at the tuning a Violin, then present the Company with a Hornpipe, and so dance a Jig through the Keyhole.

MARTIN - Thou art the Devil's Son; for he is the Father of Lyars.

OLD LAROON - Thou art the Devil's Footman, and wearest his proper Livery.

JOURDAIN - Fy upon you, Mr. Laroon; Fy upon you.

MARTIN - Mr. Laroon! O surprizing Effect of Possession—Here is no Body.

JOURDAIN - Can I not believe my Eyes?

MARTIN - Can you not! no—you are to believe mine. The Eyes of the Laity may err, the Eyes of a Priest cannot.

JOURDAIN - And do I not see Mr. Laroon and his Son!

MARTIN - You see neither. It is the Spirit within you that represents to your Eyes and Ears what Objects it pleases.

JOURDAIN - Oh! miserable Wretch.

OLD LAROON - Agad I'll try whether I am no Body or no, and whether I cannot make this Priest sensible that I am somebody.

YOUNG LAROON - For Heaven's sake, Sir, consider the Consequence.

OLD LAROON - Consequence! Do you think I'll suffer a Rascal to prove me nothing at all to my Face?

JOURDAIN - And is it possible all this is a Vision?

MARTIN - Retire to Rest—while I by the Force and Battery of Prayer, expel this dreadful Guest.

JOURDAIN - Oh! what a miserable Wretch am I!

SCENE VII

OLD LAROON, YOUNG LAROON, MARTIN.

OLD LAROON - Hearkee, Sir, will you please to tell me what this great Impudence of yours means? and what you would intend by Annihilating me.

MARTIN - It were happy for such Sinners that they cou'd be annihilated: It were worth you two hundred thousand Masses, take my Word for it.

OLD LAROON - It were happy for such Rascals as you, Sirrah, that all Honesty was annihilated.

YOUNG LAROON - But pray, Father, what Reasons have you for preventing my Match with Isabel?

MARTIN - Reasons, young Gentleman, that are not proper for your Ears. Isabel is intended for a better Bridegroom than you.

OLD LAROON - How, Sirrah! how! Do you disparage my Son? Do you run down my Boy? Hearkee, either make up Affairs between them immediately, exert thy self in thy proper office and hold the Door, or I'll blow up thy
Convent; I'll burn your Garrison, and disband such a Set of black Locusts as shall rob and pillage all Toulon.

MARTIN - I contemn thy Threats. The Saints defend their Ministers.

OLD LAROON - The Saints defend their Ministers! the Laws defend them: St. Wheel, and St. Prison, and St. Gibbet, and St. Faggot; these are the Saints that defend you. If you had no Defence but from the Saints in the other World, you wou'd few of you stay long in this. If you had no other Arms than your Beads, you would have shortly no other Food.

MARTIN - Oh Slanderous! Oh impious! some Judgment cannot be far off.

OLD LAROON - When a Priest is so near—Sirrah!

SCENE VIII

ISABEL, to them.

MARTIN - Daughter, fly from this wicked Place; the Breath of Sin has infected it, and two Gallons of Holy Water will scarce purify the Air.

ISABEL - Oh! Heavens! What's the Matter, Father?

OLD LAROON - Why the Matter is, this Gentleman in Black here, for Reasons best known to himself, and another Gentleman in Black, has thought fit to forbid your Marriage.

ISABEL - What the Saints please.

OLD LAROON - Hoity-toity! What, has he fill'd your Head with the Saints too?

ISABEL - Oh Sir! I have had such Dreams.

OLD LAROON - Dreams! Ha, ha, ha: The Devil's in it, if a Girl just going to be married should not have Dreams. But they were Dreams the Saints had nothing to do with, I warrant you.

ISABEL - Such Visions of Saints appearing to me, and advising me to a Nunnery.

OLD LAROON - Impossible! Impossible! for I have had Visions too: I have been order'd by half a Dozen Saints to see you married with the utmost Expedition; and a very honest Saint, whose Name I forget, came to me about an Hour ago, and swore heartily if you were not married within this Week, he'd lead you to Purgatory in a Fortnight.

MARTIN - Oh! grievous!

ISABEL - Can there be such Contradictions?

OLD LAROON - Pshaw! Pshaw! Yours was a Dream, and so to be understood backwards; Mine, a true Vision, therefore to be believ'd. Why, Child, I have been a famous Seer of Visions in my Time. Wou'd you believe it? While I was in the Army, there never was a Battle, but I saw it some time beforehand. I have had an intimate Familiarity with the Saints, I know them all: There is not one of them cou'd be capable of saying such a thing.

ISABEL - Oh! Sir, I saw, and heard, and must believe, for none but the Church can contradict our Senses.

OLD LAROON - So, so! the Distemper's hereditary, I find: the Daughter is as full of the Church as the Father. Come away, Son, come away: I would not have thee marry into such a Family, I shou'd be Grand-father to a Race of greasy Priests. 'Sdeath! this Girl will be brought to bed of a Pope one Day or other.

ISABEL - 'Tis out, 'tis out.

MARTIN - Oh prodigious! That such a Saint shou'd prophesy Truth through those Lips, whence the Devil has been thundring so many Lyes.

OLD LAROON - What Truth, Sir, what Truth?

ISABEL - Oh! Sir, the Blessing you mentioned, has been promised me! I am to give a Pope to the World.

OLD LAROON - Are you so, Madam? He shall have no Blood of mine in him, I'm resolv'd I'll never ask Blessings of a Grandson. Come away, Jack, come a way, I say; let us leave the Devil's Son, and the Pope's Mother together.

YOUNG LAROON - Remember, my Isabel, I only live in the Hopes of seeing you mine.

SCENE IX

MARTIN, ISABEL.

MARTIN - It were better thou shouldst howl in Purgatory ten thousand Years, than ever see that Day. Oh! that we had but an Inquisition in France. Burning four or five hundred such Fellows in a Morning would be the best way of deterring others. Religion loves to warm it self at the Fire of a Heretick.

ISABEL - Fire is as necessary to keep our Minds warm as our Bodies, Father; and burning a Heretick is really a very great Service done to himself; a Faggot is a Purge for a sick Soul, and a Heretick is obliged to the Priest who applies it.

MARTIN - There spoke the Spirit of Zeal: Let me embrace thee, my little Saint; for such thou will be, let me kiss thee with the pure Affection of a Confessor—Ha! there is something Divine in these Lips, let me taste them again; are you sure you have drank no Holy Water this Morning?

ISABEL - None, upon my Word.

MARTIN - Let me smell a third time. There. Numero Deus impare gaudet. Depend on it, Child, very great Happiness will attend you. But be sure to observe my Directions in every thing.

ISABEL - I shall, Father. I did as you commanded me this Morning.

MARTIN - Well, and did you perceive any great Alterations in your self? Any extraordinary Emotion?

ISABEL - I cannot say I did.

MARTIN - Hum! Spirits have their own Times of Operation; which must be diligently watch'd for. Perhaps your good Genius was at that Time otherwise employ'd. Repeat the Ceremony often, and my Life on the Success. Let me see, about an Hour hence will be a very good Season. Be ready to receive him, and I firmly believe, the Spirit will come to you.

ISABEL - Oh lud! Father, I shall be frightned out of my Wits at the Sight of a Spirit.

MARTIN - You will see nothing frightful, take my Word for it.

ISABEL - I hope he won't appear in any horrible Shape.

MARTIN - Hum—That is to be averted by Ave Maries. As this is a friendly Spirit, I dare say, you may prevail on him to take what Shape you please. Perhaps your Father, or if you cannot prevail for a Lay-man, I dare swear, you may at least, pray him into the Shape of your Confessor: and tho' I must suffer Pain on that Account, I am ready to undergo it for your Service.

ISABEL - I am infinitely obliged to my dear Father, I'll prepare my self for this vast Happiness, nothing shall be wanting on my Parr, I assure you.

MARTIN - And if any thing be wanting on mine, may I never say Mass again, or never be paid for Masses I have not said. Either this Girl has extraordinary Simplicity, or what is more likely, extraordinary Cunning; she does not seem averse to my Kisses. Why should I not imagine she sees and approves my Design. Well, I'll say this for the Sex: Let a Man but invent any Excuse for the Sin, and they are all ready to undertake it. How happy is a Priest,

Who can the blushing Maid's Resistance smother,
With Sin in one Hand, Pardon in the other.

ACT III. SCENE I

SCENE , Isabel's Apartment.

YOUNG LAROON, ISABEL.

YOUNG LAROON - Perdition seize the Villain, may all the Torments of twenty Inquisitions wrack his Soul.

ISABEL - Act your Part well, and we shall not want his own Weapons against him.

YOUNG LAROON - Sure it is impossible he can intend it—

ISABEL - Shall I make the Experiment?

YOUNG LAROON - I shall never be able to forbear murdering him.

ISABEL - You shall promise not to commit any Violence, you know too well what wou'd be the Consequence of that. Let us sufficiently convict him, and leave his Punishment to the Law.

YOUNG LAROON - And I know too well what will be the Consequence of that. There seems to be a Combination between Priests and Lawyers; the Lawyers are to save the Priests from Punishment for their Rogueries in this World, and the Priests the Lawyers in the next.

ISABEL - However, the same Law that screens him for having injured you, will punish you for having done Justice to him. [Knocking at the Door.

ISABEL - Oh! Heavens! the Priest is at the Door. What shall we do?

YOUNG LAROON - Damn him: I'll stay here and confront him.

ISABEL - Oh! No, by no means: For once, I'll attack him in his own Way; so the Moment he opens the Door, do you run out and leave the rest to me.

[She throws her self into a Chair, and shrieks. YOUNG LAROON overturns MARTIN.

SCENE II

MARTIN, ISABEL.

MARTIN - I am slain, I am overlaid, I am murdered. Oh! Daughter, Daughter, is this your patient Expectation of the Spirit?

ISABEL - It has been here: It has been here.

MARTIN - What has been here?

ISABEL - Oh! the Spirit, the Spirit. It has been here this half Hour, and just as you came in, it vanished away in a Clap of Thunder, and I thought would have taken the Room with it.

MARTIN - I thought it would have taken me with it, I am sure. Spirit indeed! There are abundance of such Spirits as these in Toulon. And pray, how have the Spirit and you employed your time this half Hour?

ISABEL - Oh! don't ask me: It is impossible to tell you.

MARTIN - Ay, 'tis needless too: for I can give a shrewd Guess. I suppose you like his Company.

ISABEL - Oh! so well! That I could wish he would visit me ten Times every Day.

MARTIN - Oh, Ho! And in the same Shape too.

ISABEL - Oh! I shou'd like him in any Shape, and I dare swear he'll come in any Shape too: For he is the purest, sweetest, most complaisant Spirit: I could have almost sworn it had been Mr. Laroon himself.

MARTIN - Was there ever such a—

ISABEL - Nay, when it came in first, it behaved just like Mr. Laroon, and call'd it self by his Name; but when it found I did not answer a Word, it took me by the Hand, and cry'd, is it possible you can be angry with your Laroon! I answer'd not a Word; then it kissed me a hundred times; I said nothing still; it caught me in its Arms, and embrac'd me Passionately; I still behaved as you commanded me, very passive.

MARTIN - Oh! the Devil, the Devil! Was ever Man so caught. And did you never apprehend it to be Mr. Laroon himself?

ISABEL - Heaven forbid, I should have suffered Mr. Laroon in those Familiarities, which you order'd me to allow the Spirit.

MARTIN - I am caught indeed. Damn'd driveling Idiot!   [Aside.

ISABEL - But, dear Father, tell me, shall I not see it again quickly? For I long to see it again.

MARTIN - Oh! Yes, yes—

ISABEL - I long to see it in the dark (methinks) for you know, Father, one sees Spirits best in the dark.

MARTIN - Ay, ay, you'll see it in the dark, I warrant you; but be sure and behave as you did before.

ISABEL - And will he always behave as he did before, Father?

MARTIN - Hum! Be in your Chamber this Evening at Eight; take care there be no Light in the Room, and perhaps the Spirit may pay you a second Visit.

ISABEL - I'll be sure to be punctual.

MARTIN - And passive.

ISABEL - I'll obey you in every thing.

MARTIN - Senseless Oaf. But tho' I have lost the first Fruits by her extreme Folly, yet am I highly delighted with it; and if I do not make a notable use of it I am no Priest.

SCENE III

JOURDAIN solus.

Oh! Purgatory! Purgatory! What wou'd I not give to escape thy Flames! (methinks) I feel them already. Hark! what Noise is that? Nothing—Ha! what's that I see? Something with two Heads—What can all this portend? What a poor miserable Wretch am I?

Enter SERVANT.

SERVANT - Sir, a Friar below desires to speak with you.

JOURDAIN - Why will you suffer a Man of Holy Order to wait a Moment at my Door? Bring him in. Perhaps he is some Messenger of Comfort. But Oh! I rather fear the reverse: For what Comfort can a Sinner like me expect?

SCENE IV

OLD LAROON in a Friar's Habit, JOURDAIN.

OLD LAROON - A Plague attend this House and all that are in it.

JOURDAIN - Oh! Oh!

OLD LAROON - Art thou that miserable, sad, poor Son of a Whore, Jourdain?

JOURDAIN - Alas! Alas!

OLD LAROON - If thou art he, I have a Message to thee from St. Francis. The Saint gives his humble Service to you, and bid me tell you, You are one of the saddest Dogs that ever liv'd; for having disobey'd his Orders, and attempted to put your Daughter into a Nunnery: For which he has given me positive Orders to assure you, you shall lie in Purgatory five hundred thousand Years.

JOURDAIN - Oh!

OLD LAROON - And I assure you it is a very warm sort of a Place; for I call'd there as I came along to take Lodgings for you.

JOURDAIN - Oh! Heavens! is it possible! that you can have seen the dreadful Horrors of that Place?

OLD LAROON - Seen them! Ha, ha, ha, why, I have been there half a dozen times in a Day: Why, how far do you take it to be to Purgatory? Not above a Mile and half at farthest, and every Step of the way down Hill. Seen them! ay, ay, I have seen them, and a pretty Sight they are too, a pretty tragical sort of a Sight; if it were not for the confounded Heat of the Air—then there is the prettiest Consort of Musick.

JOURDAIN - Oh! Heavens! Musick!

OLD LAROON - Ay, ay, Groans, Groans, a fine Consort of Groans, you would think your self at an Opera, if it were not for the great Heat of the Air, as I said before; some Spirits are shut up in Ovens, some are chain'd to Spits, some are scatter'd in Frying-pans—and I have taken up a Place for you on a Gridiron.

JOURDAIN - Oh! I am scorch'd, I am scorch'd—For Pity's sake, Father, intercede with St. Francis for me: Compassionate my Case—

OLD LAROON - There is but one way, let me carry him the News of your Daughter's Marriage, that may perhaps appease him. Between you and I, St. Francis is a liquorish old Dog, and loves to set People to work to his Heart.

JOURDAIN - She shall be married this Instant, the Saint must know it is none of my Fault: Had I rightly understood his Will, it had been long since performed—But well might I misinterpret him, when even the Church, when Father Martin fail'd.

OLD LAROON - I wou'd be very glad to know where I should find that same Father Martin. I have a small Commission to him relating to a Purgatory Affair. St. Francis has sentenced him to lie in a Frying-pan there, just six hundred Years, for his Amour with your Daughter.

JOURDAIN - My Daughter!

OLD LAROON - Are you ignorant of it then? Did not you know that he had debauched your Daughter?

JOURDAIN - Ignorant! oh! Heavens! no Wonder she is refused the Veil.

OLD LAROON - I thought you had known it. I'll shew you a Sight worse than Purgatory it self. You shall behold this Disgrace to the Church; a Sight shall make you shudder.

JOURDAIN - Is it possible a Priest should be such a Villain?

OLD LAROON - Nothing's impossible to the Church you know.

JOURDAIN - And may I hope St. Francis will be appeas'd.

OLD LAROON - Hum! There is a great Favourite of that Saint who lives in this Town, his Name is Monsieur Laroon. If you could get him to say half a Dozen Bead-Rolls for you, they might be of great Service.

JOURDAIN - How! Can the Saint regard so loose a Liver?

OLD LAROON - Oh! St. Francis loves an honest merry Fellow to his Soul. And hearkee, I don't think it impossible for Mr. Laroon to bring you acquainted with the Saint; for to my Knowledge, they very often crack a Bottle together.

JOURDAIN - Can I believe it?

SERVANT - Father Martin is below.

OLD LAROON - Son, behave civilly to him, nor mention a Word of what I have told you—that we may entrap him more securely.

SCENE V

MARTIN, to them.

MARTIN - Peace be with my Son. Ha! a Friar here! I like not this, I will have no Partners in my Plunder. Save you, reverend Father.

OLD LAROON - Tu quoque.

MARTIN - This Fellow should be a Jesuit by his Taciturnity. You see, Father, the miserable State of our poor Son.

OLD LAROON - I have advis'd him thereon.

MARTIN - Your Advice is kind, tho' needless. He hath not wanted Prayer, Fasting, nor Castigation, which are proper Physick for him.

OLD LAROON - Or suppose, Father, he was to go to a Ball. What think you of a Ball?

MARTIN - A Ball?

OLD LAROON - Ay, or a Wench now; suppose, we were to procure him a Wench.

MARTIN - Oh! monstrous! Oh! impious!

OLD LAROON - I only give my Opinion.

MARTIN - Thy Opinion is damnable. And thou art some Wolf in Sheep's clothing. Thou art a Scandal to thy Order.

OLD LAROON - I wish thou art not more a Scandal to thine, Brother Father, to abuse a poor old Fellow in a Fit of the Spleen here as thou dost, with a Set of ridiculous Notions of Purgatory and the Devil knows what, when both you and I know there is no such thing.

MARTIN - That I should not know thee before. Don't you know this reverend Father, Son? Your worthy Neighbour Laroon.

OLD LAROON - Then farewel, Hypocrisy. I wou'd not wear thy Cloke another Hour for any Consideration.

JOURDAIN - What do I see?

OLD LAROON - Why you see a very honest Neighbour of yours, that has try'd to deliver you out of the Claws of a roguish Priest, whom you may see too; look in the Glass and you may see an old doating Fool, who is afraid of his own Shadow.

MARTIN - Be not concerned at this, Son. Perhaps, one Hour's suffering from this Fellow, may strike off several Years of Purgatory; I have known such Instances.

JOURDAIN - Oh! Father! Didst thou know what I have been guilty of believing against thee, from the Mouth of this wicked Man?

OLD LAROON - Death and the Devil, I'll stay no longer here; for if I do, I shall cut this Priest's Throat, tho' the Rack was before my Face.

SCENE VI

MARTIN, JOURDAIN.

MARTIN - Son, take care of believing any thing against the Church: It is as sinful to believe any thing against the Church, as to disbelieve any thing for it. You are to believe what the Church tells you, and no more.

JOURDAIN - I almost shudder when I think what I believed against you. I believed that you had seduced my Daughter.

MARTIN - Oh! horrible! and did you believe it? Think not you believed it. I order you to think you did not believe it, and it were now sinful to believe you did believe it.

JOURDAIN - And can I think so.

MARTIN - Certainly. I know what you believe better than you your self do. However, that your Mind may be cleansed from the least Pollution of Thought—go say over ten Bead-Rolls immediately, go and Peace attend you—

JOURDAIN - I am exceedingly comforted within.

SCENE VII

MARTIN solus.

Go. While I retire and comfort your Daughter. Was this a Suspicion of Laroon's, or am I betrayed? I begin to fear. I'll act with Caution, for I am not able yet to discover whether this Girl be of prodigious Simplicity or Cunning. How vain is Policy, when the little Arts of a Woman are superior to the Wisdom of a Conclave. A Priest may cheat Mankind, but a Woman would cheat the Devil.

SCENE VIII - The Street

OLD LAROON, YOUNG LAROON meet.

YOUNG LAROON - Well, Sir, what Success?

OLD LAROON - Success! you Rascal! If ever you offer to put me into a Priest's Skin again, I'll beat you out of your own.

YOUNG LAROON - What's the Matter, Sir?

OLD LAROON - Matter, Sir? Why I have been laughed at, have been abused. 'Sdeath! Sir! I am in such a Passion, that I do not believe I shall come to my self again these twenty Years. That Rascal Martin discovered me in an Instant, and turned me into a Jest.

YOUNG LAROON - Be comforted, Sir, you may yet have the Pleasure of turning him into one.

OLD LAROON - Nothing less than turning him inside out. Nothing less than broiling his Gizzard will satisfy me.

YOUNG LAROON - Come with me, and I dare swear, I'll give your Revenge Content. We have laid a Snare for him, which I think it is impossible he should escape.

OLD LAROON - A Snare for a Priest! a Trap for the Devil! You will as soon catch the one as the other.

YOUNG LAROON - I am sure our Bait is good—A fine Woman is as good a Bait for a Priest-trap, as toasted Cheese is for a Mouse-trap.

OLD LAROON - Yes, but the Rascal will nibble off twenty Baits before you can take him.

YOUNG LAROON - Leave that to us. I'll warrant our Success.

OLD LAROON - Wilt thou? then I shall have more Pleasure in taking this one Priest, than in all the other wild Beasts I have ever taken.

SCENE IX

JOURDAIN, ISABEL.

ISABEL - If I don't convince you he's a Villain, renounce me for your Daughter. Do not shut your Ears against Truth, and you shall want no other Evidence.

JOURDAIN - Oh, Daughter, Daughter, some Evil Spirit is busy with you. The same Spirit that visited me this Morning, is now in you.

ISABEL - I wish the Spirit that is in me wou'd visit you, you wou'd kick this Rogue out of Doors.

JOURDAIN - The wicked Reason of your Anger is too plain. The Priest won't let you have your Fellow.

ISABEL - The Priest would have me for himself.

JOURDAIN - Oh! wicked Assertion! Oh! base Return for the Care he has taken of your poor sinful Father, for the Love he has shewn for your Soul.

ISABEL - He has shewn more Love for my Body, believe me, Sir. Nay, go but with me, and you shall believe your own Eyes and Ears.

JOURDAIN - Against the Church, Heaven forbid!

ISABEL - Will you not believe your own Senses, Sir?

JOURDAIN - Not when the Church contradicts them. Alas! How do we know what we believe without the Church? Why I thought I saw Mr. Laroon and his Son to-day, when I saw neither. Alack-a-day, Child, the Church often contradicts our Senses. But you owe these wicked Thoughts to your Education in England, that vile heretical Country, where every Man believes what Religion he pleases, and most believe none.

ISABEL - Well, Sir, if you will not be convinced, you shall be the only Person in Toulon that is not.

JOURDAIN - I will go with thee, if it were only to see how far this wicked Spirit will carry his Imposition; for I am convinced the Devil will leave no Stone unturn'd to work my Destruction.

ISABEL - I hope you will find us too hard for him and his Ambassador too.

SCENE X - Another Apartment

YOUNG LAROON in Woman's Clothes.

None ever waited with more Impatience for her Lover than I for mine. It is a delightful Assignation, but I hope it is a Prelude to one more agreeable. I shall have Difficulty to refrain from beating the Rascal before he has discover'd himself—

[Knocking at the Door.]

Who's there?   [Softly.]

BEATRICE - Isabel, Isabel.

OLD LAROON - Come in. What a soft Voice the Rogue caterwauls in.

SCENE XI

YOUNG LAROON, BEATRICE.

BEATRICE - What are you doing in the Dark, my Dear?

YOUNG LAROON - Heyday, who the Devil is this? I seem to be in a way of an Assignation in earnest.

BEATRICE - Isabel, where are you?

YOUNG LAROON - Here, Child, give me your Hand. Dear Mademoiselle Beatrice, is it you?

BEATRICE - Oh Heavens! am I in a Man's Arms?

YOUNG LAROON - Hush! hush! Don't you know my Voice—I am Laroon.

BEATRICE - Mr. Laroon! What Business can you have here?

YOUNG LAROON - Ask me no Questions, get but into a Corner of the Room and be silent, and you will perhaps see a very diverting Scene. Nay, do not be afraid, for I assure you, it will be a very innocent one; make haste, dear Madam, you will do a very laudable Action, by being an additional Evidence to the Discovery of a notorious Villain.

BEATRICE - I cannot guess your Meaning, but would willingly assist on such an Occasion.

YOUNG LAROON - Now for my desiring Lover. Ha! I think I hear him.

SCENE XII

YOUNG LAROON, MARTIN.

MARTIN - Isabel, Isabel, where are you?

YOUNG LAROON - Here.

MARTIN - Come to my Arms, my Angel.

YOUNG LAROON - I hope you are in no frightful Shape.

MARTIN - I am in the Shape of that very good Man thy Confessor, honest Father Martin. Let me embrace thee, my Love, my Charmer.

YOUNG LAROON - Bless me, what do you mean?

MARTIN - The Words even of a Spirit cannot tell you what I mean. Lead me to thy Bed, there shalt thou know my Meaning. There will we repeat those Pleasures which this Day I gave thee in another Shape—Tread softly, my dearest, sweetest! This Night shall make thee Mother to a Pope.

[YOUNG LAROON leads him out.

SCENE XIII - Another Apartment

OLD LAROON, JOURDAIN, ISABEL, A PRIEST, YOUNG LAROON, MARTIN and BEATRICE.

MARTIN - Whither would you pull me?

YOUNG LAROON - Villain, I'll shew thee whither.

MARTIN - Ha!

YOUNG LAROON - Down on thy Knees, confess thy self the worst of Villains, or I'll drive this Dagger to thy Heart.

PRIEST - He needs not confess, our Ears are sufficient Witnesses against him.

OLD LAROON - Huzzah! Huzzah! The Priest is caught, the Priest is caught.

JOURDAIN - I am Thunder-struck with Amazement.

OLD LAROON - How durst you attempt to debauch my Son, you black Rascal: I have a great Mind to make an Example of you for attempting to dishonour my Family.

PRIEST - You shall be made a severe Example of for having dishonour'd your Order.

MARTIN - I shall find another time to answer you.

OLD LAROON - Hold, Sir, hold. I have too much Charity not to cleanse you, as much as possible, from your Pollution. So, Who's there? [Enter SERVANTS.] Here take this worthy Gentleman, and wash him a little in a Horse-pond, then toss him dry in a Blanket.

FIRST SERVANT - We will wash him with a Vengeance.

ALL - Ay, ay, we'll wash him.

MARTIN - You may repent this, Mr. Laroon.

SCENE the Last

OLD LAROON, YOUNG LAROON, JOURDAIN, PRIEST, ISABEL, and BEATRICE.

PRIEST - Tho' he deserves the worst, yet consider his Order, Mr. Laroon.

OLD LAROON - Sir, he shall undergo the Punishment, tho' I suffer the like afterwards. Well, Master Jourdain, I hope you are now convinced, that you may marry your Daughter without going to Purgatory for it.

JOURDAIN - I hope you will pardon what is past, my good Neighbour. And you, young Gentleman, will, I hope, do the same. If my Girl can make you any amends, I give you her for ever.

YOUNG LAROON - Amends! Oh! She would make me large Amends for twenty thousand times my Sufferings.

ISABEL - Tell me so hereafter, my dear Lover. A Woman may make a Man amends for his Sufferings before Marriage; but can she make him amends for what he suffers after it?

YOUNG LAROON - Oh! think not that can ever be my Fate with you.

OLD LAROON - Pox o' your Raptures. If you don't make her suffer before to-morrow-morning, thou art no Son of mine, and if she does not make you suffer within this Twelve-month: Blood she is no Woman—Come, honest Neighbour, I hope thou hast discovered thy own Folly and the Priest's Roguery together, and thou wilt return and be one of us again.

JOURDAIN - Mr. Laroon, if I have err'd on one side, you have err'd as widely on the other. Let me tell you, a Reflexion on the Sins of your Youth would not be unwholesome.

OLD LAROON - 'Sblood Sir! but it wou'd. Reflexion is the most unwholesome thing in the World. Besides, Sir, I have no Sins to reflect on but those of an honest Fellow. If I have lov'd a Whore at five and twenty, and a Bottle at forty; Why, I have done as much good as I could, in my Generation; and that, I hope, will make amends.

ISABEL - Well, my dear Beatrice, and are you positively bent on a Nunnery still?

BEATRICE - Hum! I suppose you will laugh at me, if I shou'd change my Resolution; but I have seen so much of a Priest to-day, that I really believe, I shall spend my Life in the Company of a Lay-man.

OLD LAROON - Why, that is bravely said, Madam, S'bud! I like you, and if I had not resolv'd, for the Sake of this Rascal here, never to marry again, S'bud! I might take you into my Arms: And I can tell you, they are as warm as any young Fellow's in Europe—Come, Master Jourdain, this Night, you and I will crack a Bottle together, and to-morrow morning we will employ this honest Gentleman here, to tack our Son and Daughter together, and then I don't care if I never see a Priest again as long as I live.

ISABEL - [to YOUNG LAROON] Well, Sir. You see we have got the better of all Difficulties at last. The Fears of a Lover are very unreasonable, when He is once assured of the Sincerity of his Mistress,

For when a Woman sets her self about it,
Nor Priest, nor Devil can make her go without it.

Henry Fielding – A Short Biography

Henry Fielding was born at Sharpham Park, near Glastonbury, in Somerset on April 22nd 1707. His early years were spent on his parents' farm in Dorset. His family were well to do. His father was a colonel, later a general in the army, his maternal grandfather was a judge of the Queen's Bench and his second cousin would later become the fourth Earl of Denbigh.

He was educated at Eton where he became lifelong friends with William Pitt the Elder.

An early romance ended disastrously and with it his removal to London and the beginnings of a glittering literary career. Early advice on this came from another cousin, the noted poet, Lady Mary Wortley Montagu. Fielding published his first play, at age 21, in 1728.

Later that same year he journeyed to the University at Leiden, the oldest University in Holland, to study classics and law. However, within months, with funds low, mainly due to his father cutting off his allowance, he was forced to return to London and to write for the theatre.

It was a twist of fate that was to ensure him both notoriety and a reputation that would exceed his wildest expectations.

He was prolific, sometimes writing six plays a year, but he did like to poke fun at the authorities. His plays were thought to be the final straw for the authorities in their attempts to bring some sense of order to an increasingly provocative Theatre. Some of the plays denigrated, insulted, or criticised either the King, or his Government, in ways that caused them to react with their preferred response; a new law. Although the Golden Rump was cited as the play on which the authorities based their need for better regulation it is thought that the constant stepping over the line by Fielding in his own works was the actual trigger for, and target of, the new law. No copy of the play, The Golden Rump, exists today and it seems never, in fact, to have been performed or perhaps even published. Various accounts attribute Fielding as the author and others say it was secretly commissioned by Walpole himself to bring about the conditions necessary to bring the Act before Parliament.

Whatever the validity in 1737 The Theatrical Licensing Act was passed. At a stroke political satire was almost impossible. Fielding much admired – and reviled – for his savaging of Sir Robert Walpole government was rendered mute. Any playwright who was viewed with suspicion by the Government now found an audience difficult to find and therefore Theatre owners now toed the Government line, works only being available for performance after review by the Lord Chamberlain. A process that was to last in England, although greatly amended in 1843, until 1968.

Fielding was practical in the circumstances and ironically stopped writing to once again take up his career in the practice of law. He became a barrister after studying at Middle Temple – he completed the six year course in only three. By this time he had also married Charlotte Craddock, his first wife, and they would go on to have five children, but only a daughter would survive. Charlotte died in 1744 but was immortalised as the heroine in both Tom Jones and Amelia.

As a businessman Fielding lacked any financial education and he and his family often endured bouts of poverty. He did however find a wealthy benefactor in the shape of Ralph Allen, who was to later feature in the novel Tom Jones as the character foundation for Squire Allworthy.

Fielding never stopped writing political satire or satires of current arts and letters. The Tragedy of Tragedies, for which Hogarth designed the frontispiece, had, for example, some success as a printed play. He also contributed a number of works to journals of the day as well as writing for Tory periodicals, usually under the name of "Captain Hercules Vinegar". His choice of name reveals his style. But then again his other later nom de plumes are also revealing; Sir Alexander Drawcansir and Scriblerus Secundus

In 1731 Fielding wrote "The Roast Beef of Old England", which is used by the Royal Navy and the United States Marine Corps. It was later arranged by Richard Leveridge.

During the late 1730s and early 1740s Fielding continued to air his liberal and anti-Jacobite views in satirical articles and newspapers. He was nothing if not passionate and this adherence to principles would eventually have great reward for him.

Fielding was much put out by the success of Samuel Richardson's Pamela, or Virtue Rewarded. His reaction was to spur him into writing a novel. In 1741 this first novel, Shamela, was a success, an anonymous parody of Richardson's melodramatic novel. It is a satire that follows the model of the famous Tory satirists of the previous generation; Swift and Gay.

On the tail of this success came Joseph Andrews in 1742. Begun as a parody on Pamela's brother, Joseph, it swiftly developed and matured into an accomplished novel in its own right and marked the entrance of Fielding as a major English novelist.

In 1743, he published a novel in the Miscellanies volume III (which was, in fact, the first volume of the Miscellanies). This was The History of the Life of the Late Mr Jonathan Wild the Great. Sometimes this is cited as his first novel, as he did indeed begin writing it before Shamela, but it is now placed later. Once again Fielding returns to satire and one of his favourite subjects – Sir Robert Walpole. In it he draws a parallel between Walpole and Jonathan Wild, the infamous gang leader and highwayman. He implicitly compares the Whig party in Parliament to a gang of thieves, whose leader, Walpole, lives only for his desire and ambition to be a "Great Man" (a common epithet for Walpole) and should culminate only in the antithesis of greatness: being hung from a gallows. By now Walpole had resigned as Prime minster after some 20 years. Fielding could now re-affirm political allegiance back to the Whigs and would now denounce both Tories and Jacobites in his writings.

Although Fielding was never afraid to court controversy he published his next work anonymously in 1746, and perhaps with good reason. The Female Husband, a fictionalized account of a sensational case of a female transvestite who was tried for duping another woman into marriage. This was one of a number of small published pamphlets at sixpence a time. Though a minor item in both length and his canon it shows Fielding's consistent interest and examination of fraud, sham, and masks but, of course, his subject matter was rather sensational.

In 1747, three years after Charlotte's death and ignoring public opinion, he married her former maid, Mary Daniel, who was pregnant. Mary bore him five children altogether; three daughters, who died early and sons William and Allen.

Undoubtedly the masterpiece of Fielding's career was the novel Tom Jones, published in 1749. It is a wonderfully and carefully constructed picaresque novel following the convoluted and hilarious tale of how a foundling came into a fortune.

Fielding was a consistent anti-Jacobite and a keen supporter of the Church of England. This led to him now being richly rewarded with the position of London's Chief Magistrate. The position itself had no salary attached but he refused all manner of bribes during his tenure, which was most unusual. Fielding continued to write and his career both literary and professional continued to climb.

In 1749 he joined with his younger half-brother John, to help found what was the nascent forerunner to a London police force, the Bow Street Runners. (He and his siblings were quite some partnership. His younger sister, Sarah, also became a well known novelist)

His influence here was undoubted. He and John did much to help the cause of judicial reform and to help improve prison conditions. His pamphlets and enquiries included a proposal for the abolition of public hangings. This was not, as you would think because he was opposed to capital punishment as such—indeed, for example, in his 1751 presiding over the trial of the notorious criminal James Field, he found him guilty in a robbery and sentenced him to hang.

In January 1752 Fielding started a fortnightly periodical titled The Covent-Garden Journal, which he would publish under the colourful pseudonym of "Sir Alexander Drawcansir, Knt. Censor of Great Britain" until November of the same year. In this periodical, Fielding directly challenged the "armies of Grub Street" and the other periodical writers of the day in a conflict that would eventually become the Paper War of 1752–3.

Fielding then published, in 1753, "Examples of the interposition of Providence in the Detection and Punishment of Murder, a work in which, rejecting the deistic and materialistic visions of the world, he wrote in favour of the belief in God's presence and divine judgement, arguing that the rise of murder rates was due to neglect of the Christian religion. In 1753 he would add to this with Proposals for making an effectual Provision for the Poor.

Fielding's ardent commitment to the cause of justice as a great humanitarian in the 1750s unfortunately coincided with a rapid deterioration in his health. Such was his decline that in the summer of 1754 he travelled, with Mary and his daughter, to Portugal in search of a cure. Gout, asthma, dropsy and other afflictions forced him to use crutches. His health continued to fail alarmingly.

Henry Fielding died in Lisbon two months later on October 8th, 1754.

His tomb is in the city's English Cemetery (Cemitério Inglês), which is now the graveyard of St. George's Church, Lisbon.

Henry Fielding – A Concise Bibliography

The Masquerade, a poem
Love in Several Masques, a play, 1728
Rape Upon Rape, a play, 1730.
The Temple Beau, a play, 1730
The Author's Farce, a play, 1730
The Letter Writers, a play, 1731
The Tragedy of Tragedies; or, The Life and Death of Tom Thumb the Great, a play, 1731
Grub-Street Opera, a play, 1731
The Roast Beef of Old England, 1731
The Modern Husband, a play, 1732
The Mock Doctor, a play, 1732
The Lottery, a play, 1732
The Covent Garden Tragedy, a play, 1732
The Miser, a play, 1732
The Old Debauchees, a play 1732
The Intriguing Chambermaid, a play, 1734
Don Quixote in England, a play, 1734
Pasquin, a play, 1736
Eurydice Hiss'd, a play, 1737
The Historical Register for the Year 1736, a play, 1737
An Apology for the Life of Mrs. Shamela Andrews, a novel, 1741
The History of the Adventures of Joseph Andrews & his Friend, Mr. Abraham Abrams, a novel, 1742
The Life and Death of Jonathan Wild, the Great, a novel, 1743.
Miscellanies – collection of works, 1743, contained the poem Part of Juvenal's Sixth Satire, Modernized in Burlesque Verse
The Female Husband or the Surprising History of Mrs Mary alias Mr George Hamilton, who was convicted of having married a young woman of Wells and lived with her as her husband, taken from her own mouth since her confinement, a pamphlet, fictionalized report, 1746
The History of Tom Jones, a Foundling, a novel, 1749
A Journey from this World to the Next – 1749
Amelia, a novel, 1751
"Examples of the interposition of Providence in the Detection and Punishment of Murder containing above thirty cases in which this dreadful crime has been brought to light in the most extraordinary and miraculous manner; collected from various authors, ancient and modern", 1752
The Covent Garden Journal, a periodical, 1752
Journal of a Voyage to Lisbon, a travel narrative, 1755

The Fathers: Or, the Good-Natur'd Man, a play, published posthumously in 1778

Other Works (Undated)
An Old Man or The Virgin Unmasked
Miss Lucy in Town, a Play, a sequel to The Virgin Unmasked
Plutus with William Young from the Greek play by Aristophanes.
The Temple Beau, a play
The Wedding Beau, a play
The Welsh Opera
Tumble-Down Dick
An Essay on Conversation, an Essay
The True Patriot, a letter

www.ingramcontent.com/pod-product-compliance
Lightning Source LLC
Chambersburg PA
CBHW060103050426
42448CB00011B/2601